4/2016

40 YEARS
From the Brink of Extinction

Photography and Text by John D. Chaney

Regular edition: ISBN: 978-1-59152-161-7
Special edition: ISBN: 978-1-59152-165-5

Published by John D. Chaney

You may order extra copies of this book by calling
Farcountry Press toll free at (800) 821-3874.

sweetgrassbooks
an imprint of Farcountry Press

Produced by Sweetgrass Books.
PO Box 5630, Helena, MT 59604
(800) 821-3874; www.sweetgrassbooks.com.

The views expressed by the author/publisher in this book
do not necessarily represent the views of, nor should be
attributed to, Sweetgrass Books. Sweetgrass Books is not
responsible for the content of the author/publisher's work.

Printed in China.

20   19   18   17   16   1   2   3   4   5

40 YEARS
From the Brink of Extinction

This book chronicles the amazing journey of survival for a species that was expected to be extinct before the end of the twentieth century.

IN THE EARLY 1970S, THERE WERE LESS THAN 450 mating pairs of American bald eagles in the lower 48 states and their numbers had been dwindling for many years. As a college student, I learned of the plight of these regal birds and determined to create a body of work that would honor the memory of what had once inspired a nation. Today, I am delighted to present this work as a tribute to their survival and to the people who helped save the American bald eagle for future generations.

I became interested in photography in elementary school and at the age of thirteen created a photography business to support my hobby. While I continued building my skills as a photographer through high school and into college, my fascination with eagles didn't begin until I was nearly finished with my degree, majoring in Computer Science and Business Administration. My inspiration was a gift from Doc Wannamaker, one of my favorite professors. Doc was one of those teachers who had a profound impact on his students. You know the kind I'm talking about, the ones who love teaching and sharing their enthusiasm for their subject with their students. Even when you have no interest in the subject, they grab your attention and make you want to go to class because their passion is somehow contagious. Doc was so popular that some of the alums got together and donated money for a new science building that they named after him.

I met Doc Wannamaker as soon as I started college. I was

the photography editor of the newspaper and yearbook and the sports photographer, and he was the advisor for the photography program. We spent quite a bit of time together and I both liked and respected him. My junior year, I still needed a biology class to complete my core requirements, so I enrolled in one Doc Wannamaker was teaching. Doc was the first environmentalist and conservationist I'd ever gotten to know. He spent about a third of the time in that biology class talking about evolution and extinction of different species. Doc showed us pictures of animals that

them to lay thin-shelled eggs that cracked before the chicks could hatch. Further, industrialization led to pollution of many of our lakes and rivers, contaminating the eagles' food supplies. I hadn't seen a live bald eagle at that point, but the idea of its extinction and our part in it made an impact on me.

Doc knew that strong legislation could help protect animals by changing human behavior, so he told his students about a bill that was being debated in Congress. He encouraged us to petition our congressional representatives and senators to pass the

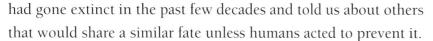

I hadn't seen a live bald eagle at that point, but the idea of its extinction and our part in it made an impact on me.

had gone extinct in the past few decades and told us about others that would share a similar fate unless humans acted to prevent it.

One of the species that Doc thought would be extinct in the next decade was the American bald eagle. Doc told us that when the bald eagle was adopted as our national symbol in 1782, they were fairly common. Over the years, people caused most of the problems that were driving them to extinction. Though bald eagles mainly eat fish and carrion, they were thought to be harmful to domestic livestock, so farmers and ranchers shot many of them. In some areas, salmon fishermen who thought the eagles threatened their livelihood awarded bounties for dead eagles and killed more than 100,000 from 1917-1953. The eagles' nesting sites were destroyed by both the logging industry and by expansion as humans built more roads and cities. DDT, an agricultural pesticide, played the most significant role in decimating the bald eagle population. Sprayed throughout the United States to control mosquitoes and other insects, DDT made its way into the aquatic food chain, accumulating in fish—the primary food for bald eagles. The pesticide built up in the eagles and caused

Endangered Species Act. As college students, we were eager to get involved and Doc provided the names and addresses of our legislators. Each of us sent hand-written letters to the people who could act on our behalf. We also included pictures of species that had recently become extinct during Doc's lifetime, such as the California and Mexican grizzly bears and the Cascade mountain wolf. (This was all before email and, typically, congressmen actually read letters from their constituents and passed laws that were important to the people who had elected them.) Doc told us about other professors around the country who were also spreading the word.

Our voices, together with those of thousands of other concerned citizens and environmentalists, were heard, and Congress passed the Endangered Species Act in 1973. In addition to setting up guidelines for federal agencies, this act made matching funds available to states with cooperative agreements and made plants and invertebrates eligible for protection.

One afternoon during my junior year, I was sitting on one of the bluffs adjacent to our campus when I saw my first bald eagle flying down the Mississippi River toward me. Unfortunately, I didn't have my camera with me, but I immediately ran to tell Doc Wannamaker what I'd seen. Since there were only about 450 mating pairs of bald eagles in the lower forty-eight states at the time, Doc made me describe what I'd seen in great detail before he believed me.

Doc was very passionate about endangered animals. He began asking me what I was going to do with my talent for photography.

time as possible looking for the scarce bald eagle. Prior to the Internet, with only word of mouth as a source for locating bald eagles, my quests were often fruitless. Most places in those days where an eagle had been spotted meant, literally, one eagle. By the 1990s, people would see two or three in a general area; by the turn of the century, there would be dozens. And the population continues to grow.

Those first trips went something like this: I'd find myself on

> *Most places in those days where an eagle had been spotted meant, literally, one eagle. By the 1990s, people would see two or three in a general area; by the turn of the century, there would be dozens.*

Up to that point, I had used photography as a means to an end, a way to help pay for some of my expenses through college. When Doc suggested that I could do something more by becoming passionate about my subjects, I had an epiphany. Up to that point, I'd taken pictures of interest to other people. The idea of photographing only things that meant something to me gave photography a whole new meaning. He suggested that I might capture the essence of this magnificent creature on its way to extinction for those who would never get to see it. For months, I went back to the bluffs of the Mississippi looking for that eagle, longing to take my first photograph of real importance. It wasn't to be. I didn't get my first picture of a bald eagle until a few years after I graduated. The American bald eagle was added to the endangered list on July 4, 1976.

Though my life got busy with work and family, I never forgot what I'd learned from Doc Wannamaker. On many business trips and personal trips with the family, I found time to break away and take pictures. Any time I was in an area where eagles had been seen, I eagerly gathered my camera gear and spent as much

a trip to an area of the country where I'd heard of a bald eagle sighting. Often, directions from those who'd seen the eagle were vague. I knew that eagles are typically found near a body of water such as a lake or river. I'd drive to what I thought was the right area, pull to the side of the road, and listen for the eagle's cry. Frequently, I would hike for long distances through rough terrain, carrying bulky camera gear.

The distinctive sound of the eagle was my clue to its location. You can hear the sound for almost a mile. Eagles can spend hours on a branch waiting for the right moment to swoop down for the perfect catch. Sometimes, I could hear the lone eagle but never see it because of the density of the forest.

Other trips, I could see an eagle on the other side of the river, but I had no ability to get there. I would wait for hours hoping the eagle would fly to my side of the river, only to watch at a great distance as the eagle moved from tree to tree out of range for my lens. Even today, with some of the most sophisticated camera equipment and extremely long lenses, I may see many eagles in the trees across a river, but they are still too far away for a good

picture. Luckily for me, many of them do fly up and down the river and actually land close enough for my camera.

When I took up photography as a kid, I enjoyed focusing on my subject and making sure I got only what I wanted in the picture. Once I got a good camera, my entrepreneurial spirit gave me the drive to make a business out of my hobby. After college, viewing photography as a means of self-expression, sharing values, telling stories, and making a difference, I began to see exactly what Doc Wannamaker had in mind for me.

bald eagle started small but continued to build year after year, and I was rewarded with exciting new images to share.

Passion for me was a personal, lonely journey in the beginning. I was able to share the results with others, but the drive came from deep within. I wanted to accomplish something and set lofty goals to achieve that end, regardless of the work and sacrifice required. As the years went by, my photography skills improved along with technology, and my goals expanded even further. With each new photograph, the drive to capture some-

I had learned one of the most valuable lessons of my life: being passionate about what you do produces excitement, joy, and a sense of fulfillment.

I finally got my first eagle picture in the early 1980s while in Alaska on a trip to photograph bears. I felt a thrill I'd never experienced while running my little company, Snap-It Photo Services. I'd captured an image of a living being that I believed many people would never get the chance to see in their lifetime and one that might actually be gone from the planet before my children were grown. I was lucky—my first eagle picture was of one in flight with a salmon in its claws, about 200 to 300 yards from where I stood. I spent the next 30 years taking pictures of the behaviors that preceded what I'd captured in that first image. The more pictures I took of these intriguing raptors, the more I learned to respect and value them. I had learned one of the most valuable lessons of my life: being passionate about what you do produces excitement, joy, and a sense of fulfillment. I've tried to carry a sense passion into everything that was important to me. As an example, being passionate about a job was more important than the compensation. Ultimately, the passion was rewarded with proper compensation. My passion for the American

thing extraordinary seems to get stronger. Through meeting with other photographers and sharing my work in galleries and with friends and associates, I've also found that just being in the world and living that passion can ignite it in others.

My photography trips have provided both excitement and lots of opportunities for learning. On one trip to Redoubt, Alaska, I took along my son Peter. We were traveling by boat down an inlet near a stream when I saw an eagle about seventy-five yards from the boat. I was so excited about seeing an eagle in a tree that close, I didn't notice a bear getting into the water to catch a salmon a mere fifteen feet from our boat. Peter redirected my attention, but not before I got my picture!

One year, I was planning to take some fellow photographers on a trip to photograph eagles, so I went to Homer, Alaska, to do some onsite planning. I'd heard stories about the Eagle Lady of Homer, Jean Keene, who had started feeding a couple of eagles in the winter of 1977. Over the years, more and more eagles showed up and she continued to feed them all. I had high expectations for that trip, but it was too early in the winter and I saw only one eagle. Unfortunately, it was perched atop a telephone pole in the parking lot of the hotel where I was staying. I spent hours trying to take pictures of that lone eagle, hoping they would look interesting enough to get more people to sign up for the trip. True to form, the eagle remained in position for a really long time, and I didn't get the image I wanted of him soaring in the sky.

Throughout the years that I have been photographing eagles,

the various festivals, I saw dozens of eagles, then years later, hundreds. Today, their numbers are in the thousands. These festivals support protecting the local environment to maintain the eagles' food sources. They also provide guidance to visitors on proper behavior to avoid disturbing eagles and their environment so the birds will remain in the area.

On my very first trip to the annual Alaska Bald Eagle Festival in Haines, Alaska, I arrived in Juneau on a Thursday night,

Laws protecting the bald eagle include protection of their nesting sites. That is very important because eagles return to their same nests year after year, often for as long as thirty-five years.

humans have done much to reverse their decline. In addition to banning DDT in 1972, we cleaned up our lakes and rivers and wrote laws to control pollution, thereby protecting the eagles' food sources. Laws protecting the bald eagle include protection of their nesting sites. That is very important because eagles return to their same nests year after year, often for as long as thirty-five years. When a mating pair's nest is destroyed, they often do not build another one. Other efforts to assist bald eagles included restoring and introducing captive-bred eagles back to areas where they had been eliminated.

Over the past few decades, eagle festivals have become common. I attend and support these functions, designed to help preserve our national symbol. Typically, the eagle festivals are located in an area near a phenomenon in nature that attracts eagles. As an example, a section of a river might have hot spring water feeding into the river, causing salmon to spawn later in the season. Another might be where the headwaters freeze and a river drops several feet, trapping fish in pools. During my early trips to

planning to charter a small Cessna to Haines the next morning. When I arrived at the charter airline office, I was informed that Haines was snowed in and no flights were going in or out for the next day or so. Several other photographers at the airport had the same goal of getting to Haines for the festival. Even the ferry was not running for the next two days, so that option was out. After a half day's wait, I went looking for an alternative. I located a freight helicopter and asked the pilot if he could fly safely in the bad weather to Haines. He assured me that he could. I went back to the group of photographers and asked if they wanted to split the cost. They agreed, and eight of us sat on the cargo floor for the short thirty-minute flight to Haines. We landed in about two feet of snow on the end of the runway, and the pilot helped us off and waved as he flew away. We walked about a quarter mile to the small airport hangar to find that it was closed and locked. There were no people in sight, so we walked to the road and after a considerable amount of time we hailed a passing truck. One of us rode into town with our rescuer to find trans-

portation to the small village of Haines for the rest of the group.

A few years later on another trip to Haines for the Bald Eagle Festival, I was driving along the side of the Chilkoot River headed back to town when I spotted a small group of eagles close to the river's edge. It was late and it had been snowing quite heavily, but there was still some light left, so I pulled the car to the side of the road to take a few pictures. I got some nice shots, but when I tried to leave, the tires had no traction and the car kept sliding closer and closer to the bank dropping into the river. The sun

it was bringing. When I woke up the next morning and opened the door, I was greeted by a wall of snow up to my chest. I got through that to find my car buried under about four feet of fresh powder. With no phone service and only a bag of Oreos for food, I had to wait to be rescued. Several hours went by before I saw another soul. My cabin was at the top of a steep driveway, about 100 yards from the road into town. Eventually, I heard a snowplow on the lower road and made my way down to talk with the driver. He committed to come back at the end of his shift

The primary food source for eagles is fish, particularly salmon. Occasionally, they will go after waterfowl.

was setting rapidly, there was no cell service, and passing traffic was sparse. I was beginning to worry that I would have to spend the night there in my car in ten-degree weather. I dared not continue to try to move the car by myself because an evening swim in frigid water was definitely not in my plans! Finally, a school bus driver spotted me and stopped to help. He told me I wasn't the first photographer to get stuck like that. He attached chains to the car and tried to pull me out, but it didn't work. As we were standing there trying to figure out what to do next, another local person in a truck came along and stopped to give us a hand. With both the bus and truck pulling, we got the car to the highway and I made it back to town. I was sure grateful those men came along when they did and were kind enough to stop in terrible conditions to help a stranger.

On another trip, I was able to rent a nice log cabin about twenty minutes from town near an area known for eagle activity. Since I was closer to my cabin, I was able to spend more time from sun up to sun down photographing the eagles. I knew a storm was approaching, but I had no clue about the amount of snow

and plow the 100 yards to the back of my car to get me moving. At least this time, I had a comfortable room with heat!

While photographing eagles in Canada, I took a boat tour along with some other photographers. One of the passengers in the boat was talking about the eagles he'd seen that day and what beautiful white feathers they had. I overheard some other photographers lamenting that the most active pictures they'd gotten that day were not of eagles with those elegant white feathers, but only those "dirty eagles." They said they couldn't understand how those eagles got so dirty. I laughed silently as I listened to the guide explain that it takes four to five years for eagles to get their white head and tail feathers, so the ones that look "dirty" are actually just immature.

The primary food source for eagles is fish, particularly salmon. Occasionally, they will go after waterfowl. I witnessed this unusual behavior. It is the only time that I recall cheering for the eagle's prey. A mother duck was about fifty feet from shore with her five very small ducklings. An immature eagle came out of nowhere at a high rate of speed, swooping in to take one of the ducklings.

The mother duck saw the threat before I did. She made such a noisy racket, squawking and flapping her wings, that the eagle was redirected and missed the target. Each subsequent attack, the mother duck was able to direct her ducklings to dive underwater at the right second, and the eagle was unable to make a successful catch. As the eagle continued to circle to re-attack, the mother duck had her young swim closer to the weeds along the shoreline. The eagle made about twenty dives at the ducklings without success before they were finally safe in the high weeds.

Thankfully, Congress has continued to support the Endangered Species Act by enacting significant amendments in 1978, 1982, and 1988, while keeping the overall framework of the 1973 Act essentially unchanged. In 2007, the bald eagle was delisted as an endangered species thanks to its strong recovery, with an estimated 10,000 breeding pairs in the lower forty-eight states today.

As the American bald eagle population has expanded, behavior in the species has changed. Early on, I didn't see eagles fighting one another for food, especially since I was extremely lucky to find a lone eagle to photograph. Today, with hundreds of bald eagles fishing in the same expanse of river, it is quite common to see several fighting over the same fish. After years of photographing eagles, one would think that you would have all the images that you would want. However, each year I am able to document new and exciting behavior. For example, this year I witnessed an eagle doing a complete summersault to protect his food from another eagle diving in to steal it away. I've captured eagles in just about every situation, including eagles swooping into the river, emerging with their prey, and their subsequent struggles to keep their catch long enough to eat it. I've captured a younger or stronger eagle taking a fish from a mature eagle, only to lose it to another eagle moments later. These were pictures I only dreamed of getting at the beginning of my quest, yet I still feel the desire to return again year after year. Perhaps I'll find a new place, or discover some new behavior I've not seen before. All I know right now is that my passion to photograph the bald eagle is as strong as ever.

*The female lays up to three eggs each
year; hunting, egg incubation, nest watch,
eaglet feeding, and eaglet brooding
duties are shared by both parents until
the young are strong enough to fly
at about twelve weeks of age.*

There's a story that during the American Revolution, a kettle of eagles was flying overhead during a major battle, and the soldiers who heard them above the gunfire believed they were crying out for freedom. The bald eagle is truly an all-American bird; it is the only eagle unique to North America.

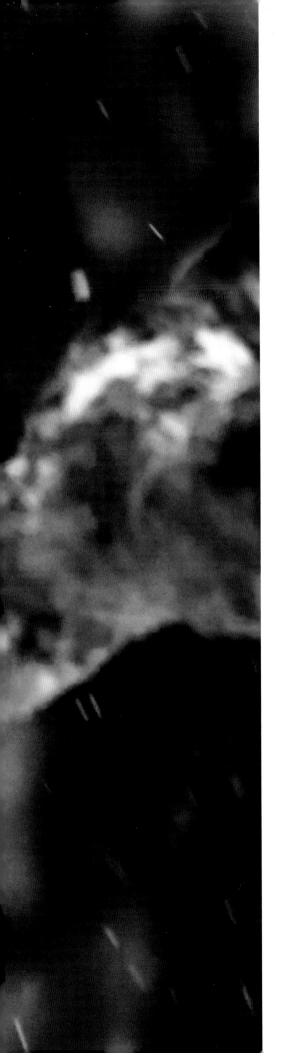

Eagles are known for their excellent eyesight. Their eyes are very large in proportion to their heads and have extremely large pupils. Eagles' eyes have a million light sensitive cells per square millimeter of retina, five times more than a human's 200,000. While humans see just three primary colors (red, blue, and green), eagles see five. These adaptations give eagles extremely keen eyesight and enable them to spot even well-camouflaged prey from a very long distance. In fact, the eagles' vision is among the sharpest of any animal, and studies suggest that some eagles can spot an animal the size of a rabbit up to two miles away!

Bald eagles are strong swimmers, but can be overcome by hypothermia if they spend too much time in extremely cold water.

Bald eagles can fly to an altitude of 10,000 feet; during level flight, they can achieve speeds of thirty-five miles per hour.

Eagles have an inner eyelid called a nictitating membrane. Every few seconds, the membrane slides across the eye, wiping dirt and dust from the cornea. Because the membrane is translucent, the eagle can see even while it is over the eye.

Several eagles soaring in a thermal together is described as a "kettle."

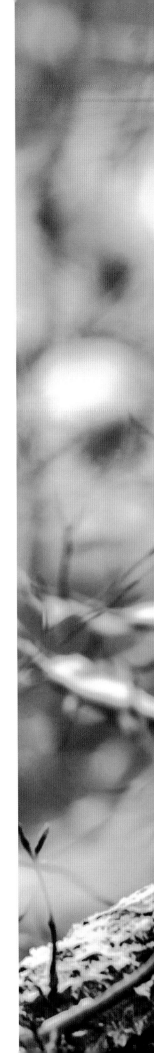

The female bald eagle stands up to thirty-seven inches tall and weighs slightly more than the male.

Bald eagles may live thirty years in the wild (even longer in captivity).

*Wingspan ranges from six
to seven-and-one-half feet.*

*Nests are often used year after year
and can weigh as much as 4,000 pounds.*

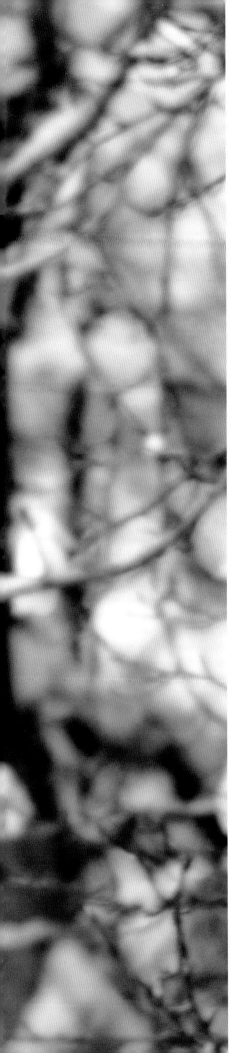

A mature eagle weighs ten to fourteen pounds and can lift up to four pounds.

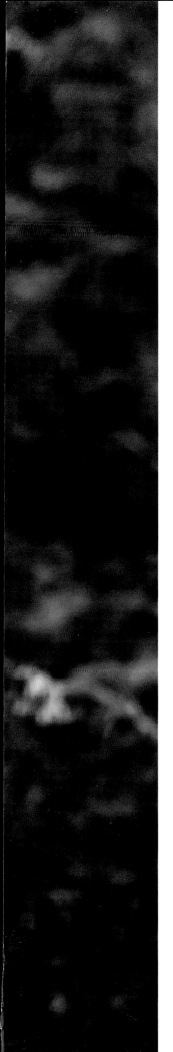

Bald eagles pair for life, but if one dies,
the survivor may accept a new mate.

In hot climates, like Louisiana and Florida,
bald eagles nest during winter.

About the Photographer

AS A TEN YEAR OLD, I KNEW I WANTED TO BE a photographer. The "Open Me First" package under the Christmas tree contained my first Brownie camera, film, flash, and flash bulbs. I took pictures of everything around me: parents, family dog and cat, friends, houses, trees, and anything else in our neighborhood. My skills improved. I read about how to take better pictures, but my Brownie didn't allow for adjustments. I needed one that had an f/stop, variable shutter speeds, and a better lens.

On my twelfth birthday, I asked for a Pentax camera, a huge step up from my Brownie. I was old enough to go to the Houston Zoo with my camera and spent many weekends taking pictures of the animals. Some of my better pictures were actually of the people looking at the animals! Thus began my fascination with photography.

I spent all of my allowance week after week on film and prints, but I couldn't afford to have all the pictures I took developed. So, I converted a half-bathroom in our house into a darkroom to do my own processing.

 I wanted to make money to support my expensive hobby, so I came up with my first business at age thirteen. I called it "Snap-It Photo Services." On day one, I'd take a roll of thirty-six pictures of houses in the neighborhood. Day two, I would develop them into 8 x 10 black-and-white photographs. Day three, I'd go door-to-door and sell them for $1 each to the respective homeowners. Day four, repeat the process.

By buying bulk film and doing my own processing, I got my cost down to about $5 for thirty-six pictures; if I sold five, I broke even, but I typically sold eighteen or twenty. After about three months, I hired some friends to help me and I paid them more than they could earn cutting grass. I learned that I was the best salesperson of the bunch, so I would take the pictures, have the other kids develop them for me, and then I would sell them. I continued this business through high school.

At the end of my freshman year, each high school in Texas nominated up to two kids to participate in a one-week photojournalism class at Trinity University in San Antonio. I was the person chosen to represent my school. My work that week was awarded

both first and second place prizes for two of my images. Because of the awards at Trinity, I was assigned the position of photo editor on both the school paper and the yearbook, positions I held through graduation.

My freshman year at Principia College, I was again given the positions of photo editor of the school newspaper and yearbook, as well as control over the school's darkroom. The athletic director asked me to be the sports photographer, which entailed traveling with the teams to take 16-mm movies of all sporting events. The photography advisor for the school was Doc Wannamaker. I made money at the school by selling group shots of sports teams, but the most money I made was selling portfolio and dress rehearsal shots for the drama department. I spent most of the money I made on more camera equipment and had some pocket money left over.

After college and the U.S. Air Force, I purchased a TeleCheck franchise, and over the next fifteen years, I continued to purchase rights to additional cities, acquire existing franchises and consolidating TeleCheck into one company. Eventually, I sold my business to a NYSE firm in 1992. When I retired in 1999, TeleCheck was very profitable, with annual revenues of about $475 million. Since then, I have divided my time between private equity and photography.

Capturing images of wild animals of all kinds has continued to fuel my passion for photography. I've learned I can tell stories with my pictures and move people to care about the animals without their being in captivity, probably one of the most important aspects of my work. I've been blessed to be able to photograph wildlife on all seven continents. I've taken pictures of bears in Alaska, Canada, and the Arctic; whales off the coast of Hawaii, South Africa, and Antarctica; and many different species of animals while on photographic safaris in Africa and the Galápagos Islands. One of my most powerful images shared on National Geographic was of an elephant mourning her dead mate by wrapping her trunk around his tusk as she stood guard for hours, keeping at bay the vultures and hyenas. ■